Remarks Upon Wayside Chapels, With Observations On The ... Chantry On Wakefield Bridge, By J.c. And C.a. Buckler

NORTH-EAST VIEW OF THE CHAPEL, ON WAKEFIELD BRIDGE.

Remarks:

upon:

Wayside : Chapels :

with : Observations : on : the :

Architecture:

and

present : state : of : the :

Chantry : on : Wakefield : Bridge :

by

John : Chessell : Buckler :

&

Charles : Buckler :
Architects:

Oxford:

John : Henry : Parker:

Rivingtons : St. Paul's : Church-yard : and : Waterloo-Place :
Weale : Architectural : Library : Holborn : London :
Stevenson : Cambridge :
M : DCCC : XLIII.

TO THE REVEREND

WILLIAM HOOPER PARKER, M.A.

RECTOR OF SAHAM TONY, NORFOLK,

LATE FELLOW OF NEW COLLEGE, OXFORD,

AND ONE OF THE

RURAL DEANS OF THE DEANERY OF BRECCLES, NORFOLK,

THIS WORK IS GRATEFULLY INSCRIBED,

BY HIS DEVOTED SERVANTS,

JOHN CHESSELL BUCKLER,

CHARLES BUCKLER.

PREFATORY REMARKS.

THE Members of the Yorkshire Architectural Society, by a recent àdvertisement for designs for the restoration of the BRIDGE-CHAPEL at Wakefield, may fairly claim the credit of having first directed public attention to these important as well as characteristic features on the lines of ancient highways.

To gain possession of this building for the sake of recovering it to Church services, has long been a favourite object with the Reverend Samuel Sharpe, Vicar of Wakefield, and the successful result of his exertions has been the means of placing the restoration under the superintendence of the Society.

The following observations upon the Chapel accompanied a set of designs, and were composed from memoranda collected within the last thirty years, during which period the writers have had opportunities of examining it, and of preserving with the pencil, the perishing forms of its architectural enrichments.

B

On the occasion referred to, it was clearly not the intention of the authors to enter very fully into the history of the subject, but merely to collect together their scattered notes; and they are not now disposed to augment the bulk of the original manuscript to any considerable extent; aware that it already forms a more detailed account than has hitherto been published by any antiquary.

It would be altogether out of place to offer any suggestions as to the manner best adapted to give stability to the walls where additional strength has become necessary, or to touch upon particulars connected with the various and difficult repairs, which are found indispensable in the present state of the building.

Whatever may be the first impression conveyed to the mind by a general review of it, touching the question of the recovery of the greater portion of its splendid detail by means of partial renewal, a close and critical examination will certainly lead to the encouraging conclusion that the main constituent features of the design have survived the combined attacks of injury and decay.

The present inquiry is strictly original, and, as such, briefly as the historical portion is treated, it will perhaps be accepted with little excuse for its publication, and be deemed not altogether an uninteresting contribution to the stock of information upon the remains of the ancient architecture of England.

As the especial purpose which the following pages were designed to serve, admitted of remarks which would prove unintelligible to the general reader without the assistance of numerous illustrative Engravings, the materials have been remodelled, with the addition of a few particulars which were not called for in the original communication.

Remarks upon Wayside Chapels, &c.

THE present inquiry is far more interesting
than may at first sight appear, these Chapels
being intimately connected with the early history of roads, which, with causeways, aque-
ducts, and bridges, had followed the Roman
eagle in its exulting flight through subjugated
provinces.

The freedom of communication, and the pene-
trating easily into different parts of the country,
were matters of importance, and no less beneficial to those who engaged in the laborious
task of commencing the work, than to the community at large.

It can scarcely be denied that the promoters
were men of true public spirit, possessed of
power, and with such a measure of property as
enabled them to execute their intentions with
success; and how complete this was we are
informed in the accounts of Glastonbury and
Muchelney, where, through the liberality and
inflexible perseverance of the Abbots, watery
wastes were redeemed by processes of draining

and embankment, and converted into fruitful and healthful districts.

Security was not overlooked, as appears by the frequent selection of swampy situations for the sites of Monasteries. The labour and expense consequent upon such undertakings were disregarded.

Industry and wealth—and both were at hand —were the means best calculated to attain the object; and experience proved in very many instances, that a luxuriant soil gathered around these splendid mansions, diffusing abundance and prosperity through the territories dependent upon them.

A permanent approach to a chosen site thus circumstanced must, in the first instance, have been formed, and then protected, and as the co-operation of multitudes was needful in a work of great and various employment, communication with places remotely situated required that these causeways should spread in various directions, and to great distances; and we can form but an imperfect notion at the present day, of the inhospitable character of the country over which, in many situations, these artificial roads were carried with such incredible labour.

Nor was it lightly considered that the means of obtaining a safe passage across wide tracts, or thinly peopled districts, and the necessity for free intercourse between cities and the larger monastic institutions, required encouragement and promotion, and early led to the systematic formation and maintenance of public ways, under the protection of religious establishments, whose possessions extended over a very considerable portion of the country; and the relics of information to be gathered of the scheme anciently adopted, of fixing Chapels along the lines, are not, even at this distant period, too few or inconsiderable to be regarded as a curious subject of investigation; and it is hoped that these brief references may lead to its further pursuit.

In the advance of national importance, the very ancient mode of communication by ferries was superseded by the construction of permanent bridges across unfordable rivers, and the recourse to these pointed out the most appropriate situations for the erection of Chapels.

Besides Bridge-Chapels there were others on the highway, or in lonely places, which linked the intervals in the chain of communication, and were founded with the same benevolent intention, of providing for the temporary rest and refreshment of pilgrims and travellers; and since journeys in former times had, perhaps, less to do with commerce than religion, it seems very probable that the road between these little asylums was entrusted to their peculiar care, the whole being directed by and under the control of the superior establishments, from which such provident measures emanated.

Although these beneficial undertakings were mainly promoted and effected through the powerful patronage or instrumentality of the clergy and religious orders, the riches of the community tended indirectly to their advancement.

The wealth of the Monasteries was accumulated by contributions from all parts of the kingdom. Their foundation or endowment might rest in the bounty of an individual, but their revenues were greatly increased by the gifts of devout strangers and pilgrims, and the generous bequests of benefactors. Thus aided, the architectural beauty of the domestic buildings, and the grandeur and magnificence of the gateways and Churches, resulted from the scientific studies nurtured by those who retired from the strife of the world to live professedly in the practice of religion, and in unremitting devotion to the good of their neighbour.

The laity by taking a due part in the maintenance of the spiritual pastors or landlords, at whose hands so many benefits were received, sustained the common welfare by the exact observance of making a portion of that which had been so freely bestowed upon them, a tribute to the impartial dispensers of good, the parents and promoters of literature and of the arts and sciences, and the main supports of the population which gathered around their noble domains.

A small Chapel was frequently situated on the outer boundary of Convents so as to be approached without entering the precinct gateway. It was also one among the uses to which the apartments over bars at the foot of bridges or the entries of a town were occasionally set apart:—

The west-gate of the city of Canterbury was an instance of this kind .

At Litcham in Norfolk the Chapel belonging to the religious house established on the bank of the Nar, and in the road to Walsingham, was attached to the foot of the bridge for the admission of all who passed by the way.

These solitary Chapels had no lodging rooms, and were places of transit rather than of sojourn: within their consecrated walls each wayworn and devotional traveller found rest for a short interval at the hours of prayer, or during a

---

ª Gostling, in his " Walk in Canterbury," has the following note in reference to this subject;—" In the time of King Richard the Second, Holy Cross Church was (as is now north-gate) over the gate, which when Archbishop Sudbury took down and rebuilt, he erected the present Church, and added a Church-yard to it, with leave of the King."

toilsome journey: here he gave utterance to
his gratitude for past mercies, and to supplica-
tions for future; and then he sped him to the
Hospital for bodily repose and refreshment—
sure of welcome from the good Superior who
"loveth the stranger in giving him food and
raiment[b]."

The clerical offices were performed by an
authorized member of the religious house in
possession of the advowson, a cappelane subservient to the parish priest, or in appointment
of the lord of the manor.

We can scarcely wonder at the scanty
supply of information on the subject of Wayside Chapels. Their name, as well as their
use, is now almost forgotten, and the remains
of these solitary little buildings though frequently to be met with, have never hitherto
excited sufficient interest to lead to any inquiry
as to the purpose for which they were formerly
erected[c].

The one at Wakefield could not escape observation, nor fail to secure admiration, on

[b] Deut. x. 18.

[c] "Entering Stia, a small town among the Appennines, with the
ruins of an old castle above it, I saw a little Chapel at the end of the
bridge, on which was an inscription to this effect :—' Here is the
bridge to enter Stia, and here is the Chapel of our Blessed Lady;
may it prove to us a bridge to Heaven !'"

account of its architectural excellencies; but its elevation to the distinction of a Chantry so far back as the reign of King Edward IV., left no chance of its being generally remembered and recognised as one among the number of the Wayside Chapels of an earlier age; certain as it is that its after dedication at the period just named, did not diminish its usefulness as a charitable foundation for the relief of weary pedestrians.

But notwithstanding this, and though the purpose of the foundation was extended in the manner above mentioned, and a proportionate increase made in its revenues by the additional endowment, yet it does not appear that any alteration of the structure followed, at least in the architecture of the exterior, whatever may have been deemed useful or appropriate in the arrangement of the interior; the latter, if required, has been entirely lost in the wreck which attended its suppression.

It is necessary to remark this, because the date of the institution of the Chantry has hitherto guided opinion as to the age of the Chapel; whereas there is not a feature in it excepting a few more recent restorations, which is not strictly original, that is, of the age of King Edward II.

It may be mentioned, that although Chan-

tries were often founded in parish Churches,
separate buildings were not always added for
the celebration of the private services, which
were performed at the Altar in the chancel;
and that the term *Chantry*, although strictly
correct in this instance, is too frequently mis-
applied.

Wayside Chapels were the only ancient places
of public worship with which burial grounds
were not locally connected.   They had no
walled enclosures, and could never have been
more alone than many are now on the highways
to Walsingham.

Those near Hillborough have been planted
on the bleak brows of elevated ground near the
roadside, and are without particular architectural distinction, being little oblong buildings
of equal breadth throughout, as plain in design
as in their figure.

The walls are roofless and broken, the cracks
and chasms serving to channel away the water
from the moss-grown summit.

The interior, which could once afford rest to
the weary, and a pittance to the distressed, is
now too desolate to be sought as a shelter by
cattle.

No marvel then that travellers in later days
have neglected to turn a few paces out of the
way to visit these ancient relics: they would

find them not altogether uninteresting, but overgrown with briars, and half filled up with heaps of old rubbish.

No kind of sepulchral memorial has been discovered within or on the outside of any of these edifices, often as death must have overtaken the pilgrim on his way.

Chances of this kind were not provided for by a consecrated space for burial, as the custom of entombing the dead around the sanctuary in which the living assembled for worship, was never extended to Wayside Chapels, neither was the administration of baptism, nor the celebration of matrimony included in the duties prescribed to them, as was sometimes the case in privileged instances in assistant Chapels belonging to districts at a distance from the mother Church.

The ruins of a village Church environed by the graves and monuments of mortality, present a less dreary aspect than these forlorn structures.

There is after all something so congenial to our feelings in the custom of thus assembling the living and the dead together, of kneeling amidst their enshrined ashes, and upon the floor covered with their venerable memorials, that we could not relinquish it but with reluctance.

Standing as many of these little Chapels do
in the most dreary and conspicuous places, on
ground so barren as to have been left to this day
without cultivation, the walls remaining unre-
moved merely because improvement has not
reached the spot they occupy, they proclaim the
danger and the necessities to which travellers in
former ages were exposed.

Surely there must have been something more
than idle curiosity in pilgrimages, conducted as
they were under many and severe privations,
without prospect of relief for many long days
together, except in the hope of assistance within
the walls of these provident institutions.

The beautiful Chapel situated on the east
side of Wakefield Bridge, and at right angles
with it, presents a bolder appearance than is
seen in other examples, not excepting the cele-
brated one of St. William of York, which,
owing to the course of the river, stood parallel
with the Ouse Bridge, two of the arches of
which, with their triangular abutment-piers,
were extended to form a basement for the
superstructure.

The original foundation was raised under
the invocation of St. Anne, the mother of the
Blessed Virgin, to whom was subsequently
dedicated the Royal Chantry, endowed after

the battle fought near the spot between the conflicting Houses of York and Lancaster, in the year of our Lord 1460[d].

The old error with respect to its true age admits, perhaps, of excuse, and can only be detected and refuted by sound architectural evidence.

The authors never remember to have heard a sufficiently high date ascribed to the building, which strongly proclaims, by every feature of its design, the period of the fourteenth century, to which it belongs.

The Bridge at Wakefield is of considerable length, and was, till within little more than half a century, a footway about sixteen feet in width between the parapets, with triangular recesses over the side piers.

Nine arches with their supporting piers were required to carry the way over the river at this place.

---

[d] Hall relates that the Duke of York's second son, the Earl of Rutland, a boy only twelve or thirteen years old, was stopped at Wakefield Bridge as he was flying with Sir Robert Aspall, his chaplain and schoolmaster.

The poor boy fell on his knees to pray for mercy, but as soon as he was known, Lord Clifford, whose father had been killed by the Yorkists at St. Alban's, plunged his dagger into his heart, vowing by God's blood that he would do the like to all of kin to York, and then the savage bade Aspall go on and tell his mother, the Duchess, what had happened.

In point of construction, adequate firmness was given to the work, but nothing attempted in the way of ornament.

The parapet has been rebuilt, and the arches have not escaped alteration beyond that which became necessary when the structure was widened on the west side, but the east still presents much of its original and venerable appearance; and here we discover that the low-browed arches consisted of four substantial, detached ribs of compact masonry, springing with perfect simplicity from their abutments.

The road ascends slightly from each extremity to the crown of the centre arch, against the northern pier of which, towards the town, the Chapel was erected, in handsome elevation above the common level.

There were formerly two or three steps from the bridge up to the doors of the Chapel, but the levels are now so far changed as to have left the floor one ample step below the pavement of the bridge.

The raised footpath has almost left the front of the building without a plinth, which was originally of handsome height, rich in mouldings, and in fine relief from the wall, breaking round all the buttresses, and uniting with the sills of the blank arches.

The basement upon which the Chapel is

raised from the bed of the river to the level of the bridge, offered no temptation to mischief, and consequently retains its pristine simplicity unimpaired ; its firm and compact condition is of the utmost importance to the permanent safety of the superstructure, which, by the care and skill of its builders, alike shewn in their choice of materials and ability in the use of them, retains a strong hold upon its massy foundations after long exposure to the excessive and repeated injuries it has suffered.

It abuts upon a pier of the bridge between two of the main arches.

The breadth at this extremity is limited to about nine feet, in order to prevent further impediment to the impetuous course of the Calder than is occasioned by the resistance of the pier itself.

This precaution has given rise to the most clever contrivances :—

The basement becomes gradually increased by a slant on each side, the impending superstructure being carried over a bold projection by means of radiating corbels.

This gain in space is surmounted by another continuous line of corbelling on each side, altogether thirty-five feet in length, and jutting forward so far towards the north and south, that the lateral walls are actually made to press

c

their entire weight upon the outer verge of the deep and finely-moulded corbels, with the exception of an inconsiderable portion at the eastern extremities, which rests in the accustomed manner on the walls beneath, beyond the point at which the necessary width for the Chapel had been acquired, without encroachment on the current's passage.

By the same ingenious application of corbels, the Chapel at Rotherham is sprung over two of the arches of the bridge, against a pier of which it is built.

Although the water washes the plinth on both sides, and sometimes rises several feet above the bank, it has never occasioned any material injury to the structure or the material of which it is built.

Stone of two different qualities has been employed.

In the plain and solid parts of the walls throughout, sandstone from the immediate neighbourhood was used, but in the windows and cornices (with slight exceptions in the latter), and the whole of the ornamental work, Roche Abbey stone.

Their resistance to the attacks of time is of course unequal, but it may be remarked that the state of the mouldings and ornaments proves that a material of superior quality could scarcely have been selected for the purpose; certainly none in which the delicacy of workmanship could have been more exquisitely defined.

Carrying the eye up from the basement to the superstructure, the attention is at once fixed by the altitude of the building; it is also much more considerable as an appendage to a bridge, than any other now remaining in England.

The famous Chapel, before referred to, on the Ouse Bridge at York, was by no means of rival dimensions.

It was of earlier date;—of the twelfth and thirteenth centuries.

To the former of these periods was to be ascribed the greater portion of its architecture, considerable as were the mutilations of the original design.

The *alteration* effected in the upper part of its walls in the thirteenth century, has sometimes been confused with the rebuilding of the bridge from the foundations, under Archbishop Walter de Grey.

Another circumstance has tended to misapprehension as to its true date—the sentence passed upon the citizens for a fatal conflict, of which the bridge was the scene.

The crime was to be atoned for by their founding a Chantry on the place of slaughter, and providing two priests to say mass therein for the souls of the slain for ever.

The demand however was not followed by exact performance.

The Bridge-Chapel, just before the date of this event, had been extensively altered and thoroughly restored, and we may suppose presented a lighter, loftier, and more pleasing exterior than anciently with its plain Norman parapets ; and set aside the obligation to build a distinct edifice for the purpose.

The then new work appears to have been raised upon the lower stage of the original fabric ; and whatever may have been the pristine aspect of the exterior of the building, the interior, in its renewed state, was probably inferior in bold enrichment, to the Norman design.

The ancients though daring in the alteration of their buildings, were in general careful to preserve and incorporate some portion of them, however inconsiderable, with the new walls.

If St. William's Chapel escaped demolition partly on account of its ancient dedication, its alteration at a time when the bridge was under re-edification, and at a period too when a great and decisive change had been effected in architectural costume, was perhaps to be expected, and was accordingly undertaken, and the new architecture engrafted upon the other at the sill-line of the windows; the north doorway, and the wall with the arcade on the inside, being preserved in all their original beauty till the final destruction both of the bridge and Chapel, at the commencement of the present century.

There could have been no rivalry between the Chapels at York and Wakefield; the former was incomparably less elaborate in design than the latter, which could never have been excelled: but it possesses claims to admiration superior to any that can result from an extraordinary display of decoration; namely, elegant proportion, symmetry, and purity of embellishment.

The detail of the exterior presents a time-worn aspect, rather than the appearance of ornament which has perished or been mutilated by violence; much that is within reach may have suffered in this way, but age, by slow process, has more extensively worn away the beautiful finish by which the sculptured elaborations were formerly distinguished; yet, even with this admission, it seems almost impossible to mistake the true character of any of the mouldings or ornaments, how much soever they may be corroded.

A defective feature or member in one place,

may be successfully sought for in another, so as to preclude a doubt of the satisfactory restoration of the Chantry.

The age of the building cannot now be distinctly ascertained from historical records, and where these fail, the architecture invariably proves a valuable guide.

On this authority it may be ascribed to the beginning of the fourteenth century in the reign of King Edward II.

But perhaps something more than an unsupported opinion will be expected on this point.

The curvilinear forms throughout the detail of the Chapel would, alone, afford decisive evidence of its age.

All the perpendicular shafts stop at the springing line of the arches and tracery, and thence immediately curve off to form the different patterns.

This particular constituted one of the chief characteristics of the most magnificent of all the styles of Pointed Architecture; and led to the production of many glorious designs, in which wonderful taste, ingenuity, and skill, were exhibited in windows and other ornamental features.

The style here spoken of commenced in the reign of King Edward I. and was superseded in that of King Edward III. by whose power-

ful patronage William of Wykeham, Bishop of
Winchester, was enabled fully to exercise his
genius as an Architect, and in whose works,
which were distinguished by stateliness of character and magnificent proportion, the *curvilinear* form, as a leading character, was abandoned for the straight, or *rectilinear*, extending
uninterruptedly into the arches and separating
them into spaces, within each of which a pattern was formed, the whole beautifully arranged
and connected, and made to compose a sym-
metrical design.

The transition just described as tending
towards a change in the characteristic varieties
of architecture so as to produce a new style,
in establishing which the above-named Prelate
was mainly instrumental, might be shewn by
reference to many contemporaneous specimens.

The union of upright with curvilinear lines
obtained for a time; at length the latter were
relinquished, the arch only being retained in
the composition of tracery.

The ancient east window of the chancel of
St. Aldate's Church, Oxford, was a most singular example of the intermediate kind.

It consisted of five compartments, the mullions being carried in continuous parallel lines
from the sill to meet the enclosing arch.

The tracery within each division was less

substantial than the uprights, and presented diversified patterns, each of considerable elegance; but an harmonious whole would not have remained upon the removal of the perpendicular shafts by which they were intercepted.

This singular window was restored a few years since, but the copy has lately been replaced by another derived from earlier authority.

The ball-flower in the cornice of the west front should not be allowed to pass unnoticed among the characteristic ornaments of the period to which the Wakefield Chantry is here referred.

The absence of authentic information as to the precise date is the more to be regretted, as we are left without a clue to the Founder, whose name perhaps might have excited no surprise at his liberality in the performance of this pious undertaking.

He projected a work of no common character, and required for his purpose ability of superior power.

Every hand employed was guided by the first-rate skill; and the munificence of the patron encouraged the fullest exercise of a genius fruitful in invention and happy in adaptation.

Allusion has already been made to the origin

of these ancient and very interesting structures, of which numerous examples remain in a more or less dilapidated state, and some on a very small scale.

To this class belongs the Bridge-Chapel at Bradford, in Wiltshire.

This little room, which still retains its doorway on the footpath, and is domed over with ribbed stone-work, appears to have been partially altered or wholly rebuilt from the level of the floor.

The supporting corbels which spring from the faces of one of the angular piers, and overspread each other, finally terminating in a square platform, present perhaps an almost unequalled specimen of ingenious construction.

The Chapel at Rotherham, however, approaches nearly in point of dimensions to this of Wakefield.

Their interior measurements are respectively thirty-two feet by fourteen feet, and forty feet by sixteen feet eight inches.

The design of the Chapel at Rotherham is plain.

There have been two windows on each side, one at the east end, and one high up, and of small size, at the west end over the entrance.

The pediments and side parapets are embattled, and terminated with numerous crocketed pinnacles.

The mullions and tracery of all the windows have been destroyed; and whatever ornamental features may have graced the interior, there is nothing of the kind now visible.

The Chapel on the ancient stone bridge across the Ouse at St. Ives, Huntingdonshire, is in so decayed a condition, owing to the accidents which have happened to it, and to the alterations made in its walls since its appropriation to various mean uses, that its speedy destruction is probable.

It is a small room, built on one of the piers, jutting out on the east side, towards the centre of the bridge.

The Chapel attached to the ancient bridge between London and Southwark measured sixty feet in the clear length.

It was built by Peter Colechurch, in the twelfth century, and the east end was polygonal.

Irregular as is the form of the basement upon which the Chapel at Wakefield is built, yet the four walls meet upon it in a true rectangular figure, without distinction between sanctuary and body, the design being carried out with studied elegance and uniformity in all the features—buttresses, windows, and pinnacles.

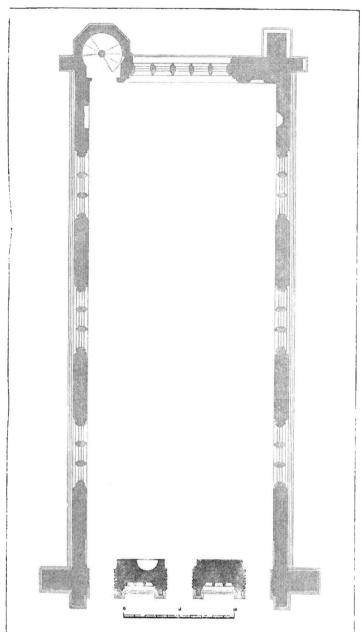

PLAN OF THE CHAPEL ON WAKEFIELD BRIDGE.

The north-east angle is varied by a graceful octagonal bell-turret, enclosing the staircase.

The parapets of the west front and sides are horizontal; that over the east end was raised into a slight pediment.

It may seem necessary to remark, that the building here described, so elegant in its character, and so beautifully ornamented, is comprehended in the space of fifty feet in length by twenty-five feet in width, and thirty-six feet in height.

The clustered pinnacles which formerly augmented the beautiful appearance of the structure, carried up the elevation considerably above the latter dimension.

There are five compartments in the width of the west front between the double buttresses on the angles, separated by slender shafts retreating in three stages, and terminating with gablets just above the line of battlements.

The arches within these exactly correspond. Three are pierced with doorways, and the whole range, uniformly adorned with ogee cornices, is surmounted with crocketed pediments, the centre more superbly enriched than the rest.

Their finials mount up to the cornice, which by a steep weathered slope, crowned with cross-looped battlements, terminates the main wall of the building, and supports the recessed parapet.

The spandrels over the arcade are occupied by tracery disposed in the most graceful patterns, springing in conjunction with the pediments, and thence branching off to occupy the entire space allotted to them; while the crockets and finials on the most prominent members, exhibit, even in their mutilated state, traces of the rich and beautiful variety of foliage of which they have been composed.

Attention may be directed to the bases from which the mullions of the two blank compartments spring. The particular is minute, but these peculiar terminations, which are now indistinct, were, rather more than a quarter of a century since, nearly perfect, and a keen eye may yet discover traces of the mouldings mitering with those of the sill.

The parapet is full of sculptures beneath triple canopies richly groined and ornamented with pinnacles, over which rise the battlements completing the design.

The west front is without a window, and contains the only external doorways the Chapel originally had.

Triple entrances, which often distinguished buildings of magnitude, present by their introduction in an edifice of the present class, a peculiarity worthy of observation.

It is to be remarked that the arches are pierced

so closely to the angles, that the stone-work of
the side walls which form their abutments, has
been recessed to receive the wooden doors, the
substance of which when opened would other-
wise have impeded the free passage to the interior.

Each of the profile or side elevations presents
three windows of a square form, sheltered with
the usual label mouldings, and completely oc-
cupying the height of the wall allotted to them
between a cornice at their sill, and the master
cornice of the building, the position of the latter
being determined by the main wall of the west
front: the same level was also preserved in
springing the original east parapet, which in
ornament agreed with those on the sides.

The broad and lofty dimensions of the Altar
window, which assumed the pedimental form
of the parapet, completely occupied the space
between the buttresses on the south angle and
the octagonal turret, the greater portion of
whose diameter is in advance of the east wall,
and being flush with the north side admits the
addition of a buttress.

Its altitude above the roof is considerable,
and the design of the parapet, which exceeds
the diameter of the walls supporting it, may be
presumed. from the remains, to have resembled
those already described.

It is to be regretted that no very ancient drawings of the Chantry have been handed down to us. Reference, however, of a highly useful kind, may be made to several works of this description which tend to elucidate our researches, viz.:—to a print by Cawthorn, another in "the Vale of Bolton," and to an original drawing by Henry Lumb of Wakefield, Esq.

The writers have only a few remarks to offer upon the print of the Chapel engraved by W. H. Toms from a drawing by Geo. Fleming, A.D. 1743.

The side windows appear to have been perfect at the time the view was taken, but, unfortunately, the artist has not defined the tracery sufficiently well to render it of any particular value.

It may be observed further, that the summit of the staircase-turret is represented as somewhat more perfect than shewn in any other drawing; and that there were then to be seen larger remains of the eastern gable than are elsewhere recorded.

The engraving in "𝕷𝖔𝖎𝖉𝖎𝖘 𝖊𝖙 𝕰𝖑𝖒𝖊𝖙𝖊" should not perhaps pass unnoticed, although it adds nothing material to our information.

All these authorities agree in representing the exterior of the Chapel in a melancholy state of ruin so lately as the year 1800, soon after which however it was partially restored.

The undertaking was creditably performed; as much of the *ancient* masonry as could be found, being collected, and carefully reinstated; no new stone-work of consequence was added, nor any thing injurious done to the character of the building, and perhaps nothing more was deemed necessary than to keep out the weather, and save the Chapel from irretrievable destruction.

By ancient masonry, the authors must not be understood to mean that it was wholly of the original building. Some valuable portions of it were assuredly of that kind, but by far the greater quantity was of coarse workmanship, and in feeble imitation of those features of the design which had decayed away, fallen down through neglect, or been demolished at the time of the suppression of Chantries.

This leads to the remark that at some period far beyond memory, a *general restoration* of the exterior of the Chapel was undertaken.

An attempt, by no means inexpensive, was made to fill up the gaps produced by age and injury, in stone-work wrought to harmonize with the original, but the intention was superior to the performance.

Several of the canopies in the parapet of the west front, and many of the battlements, may easily be recognised as of the quality alluded

to ; and to the same date must also be referred
the eastern and two side parapets, of which
the northern, at least, was afterwards by some
accident thrown down.

The wall was in this state, and the north
angle of the west end quite demolished to the
foot of the parapet, when the above drawing
and prints were made, thus proving that the
Chapel has undergone a second general restoration, which was probably not extended beyond
the labour of collecting the dispersed fragments, and refixing them in their places.

It may savour of ingratitude, but never-
theless seems far from incredible to believe that
the profits arising from the misappropriation
of the interior, enforced some regard for the
condition of the exterior :—after all, these were
only attempts to keep a ruin in repair.

The staircase-turret retained, within Mr.
Lumb's recollection, a portion of its enriched
parapet, which when it fell was never restored.

It is melancholy to recollect and record that
the superb tracery of the windows was wholly
obliterated at this time.

It had often suffered violence, and was pieced
and patched in an unsightly manner to exclude
the weather from the interior ; but yet enough
of the pattern remained to shew the beauty of
the original design.

... the same date can also be referred
... two ... of which
... at least, ... words by some
...

... date, and the more
... quite demolished to the
... ... the above draw...
... proving the
... a second general restora-
... ... not extended beyond
... collecting the dispersed frag-
... ... them in their places.

... of ingratitude, but never
... incredible to believe ...
... from the misappropriation
... the ... some regard for
... ... after all, these were
... carried ... to a pole.

... retained, within Mr
... ... a portion of its ...
... what ... it fell was never restored.

It is ... ... to recollect and ... ...
... the windows were ...
... at ...

... ... and was ...
... in ... manner ...
... to ... but ... ...
... to shew the ... ...
...

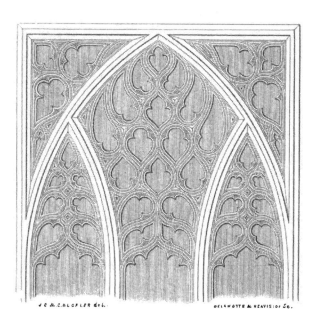

J.C. & C.H.L.GFLER del.   DELAMOTTE & HEAVIS dor SC.

TRACERY OF THE SIDE WINDOWS.

Not a vestige however was spared, even the sills were removed, half the substance of the jambs cut away, the labels on the inside destroyed, and the graceless chasms filled with the stone-work which still remains.

It is singular that not a remnant of tracery should have presented itself among the numerous fragments of carved stone-work belonging to the Chapel, brought to light at different times, within and immediately around the building.

The relics which have been recently recovered are of little value.

The last endeavour to prop up the injured walls and buttresses shews itself in the west front.

Material, such as it was, was not spared, but the addition of labour beyond that of fixing the stone, could not be endured; and the huge props of coarse masonry at once sustain and deform the building.

Whether or not these clumsy abutments have had the effect of loosening the hold the four slender buttresses previously had upon the wall, certain it is that these members have disappeared since the year 1813, when they were all in their places and quite perfect.

The present most striking deficiencies in the exterior design of the Chapel are :—the northern turret, and the crocketed pinnacle of that of the

D

southern angle of the west front; the smaller
buttresses between the doors, the mullions and
tracery of all the windows, the south-eastern
pinnacle, the parapets, and the embattled summit of the octagonal turret enclosing the staircase which ascends to the roof of the building,
and conducted to the gloomy room in the basement—a cold and seemingly comfortless cell,
scantily lighted by loop windows, and without
a fireplace; it answered the purposes of a
Sacristy, and was used by the officiating priest
during the intervals of the services at the Altar.

During the period of the misuse of this apart-
ment, a door was broken through the east wall,
for the purpose of gaining access to the small
space of ground which extends a few yards
beyond it.

Ponderous oaken beams in the ceiling support the floor of the eastern portion of the
Chapel; the western rests on a solid concrete
mass forming the remainder of the substructure.

But the catalogue of injuries remains to be
completed.

The interior presents a spectacle of unre-
strained mischief and deplorable ravage.

Every member and ornament of the architecture which stood in advance of the walls—
mouldings, corbels, cornices, buttresses, canopies, and pinnacles—has been hacked away to

prepare the surface for plaster, paper, wood-work, or whatever best suited the convenience (not to say taste) of the occupant, who was not bound to take things as he found them, and consequently did not scruple to mangle, and in places to undermine, the walls which sustained the roof over his head.

These, on all sides, have been excavated in the most barbarous manner for flues or recesses; and the wretched mode in which some of the breaches were repaired after they had served their purpose, testifies regard for common appearance rather than any desire to restore that strength of which the walls had been so unceremoniously defrauded.

Examples of groined or ceiled roofs in oak, of the date of the Wakefield Bridge-Chapel, and the reign which preceded it, are by no means common.

The shamefully desecrated eastern aisle[e] of

---

[e] This name is advisedly affixed to the aisle immediately in front of the entrance to the lady choir, to which it serves the purpose of an ante-chapel.

But besides the broad aisle just named, there is another space not nearly so large, and to the west of it, separated by a stone screen, and approached from the north and south, as well as by doorways on the sides of the high altar: this is the feretry.

The *eastern aisle of the choir* in cathedral and abbey Churches is often erroneously called the presbytery, a name which when used to designate a portion of an English church, is alone applicable to the sanctuary, choir, or chancel.

the choir of St. Alban's Abbey, however, has a panelled ceiling in the broad centre space conducting to the Lady Chapel, and a groined roof in the sides, both aptly combined with the elegant architecture of the building, and of the age of King Edward I.'

But the specimen more nearly allied than the foregoing to our present subject, is to be seen in the page's room at Penshurst.

This is a flat ceiling of oak, composed of broad ribs placed in close order, and sparingly intersected by others of equal substance in a transverse direction, uniformly wrought with

' This is one of the most handsome specimens of under-roofing in wood remaining in ancient English architecture, throughout the whole range of which there is not a single instance to be named of imitation work at all resembling those so commonly met with in Normandy, whether in regard to its own antiquity, or that of the Church in which it appears.

In the instances where the larger Anglo-Norman buildings were not groined with stone, the naked timbers, now concealed from view, have been underlined with ceilings or groined roofs many ages after the completion of the structure.

But this was not the case in Normandy, and attention should be directed to the fact, because it is not generally known, at least by English antiquaries who have described the ecclesiastical architecture of that part of France, that many of the noblest parish and monastic Churches which seem to present stone roofs groined in keeping with the pillars by which the ribs are supported, and with the rest of the design, are of plaster on wood framework, most probably of subsequent date to the fabric, but so well combined, and remaining in most cases so free from injury and decay as to have escaped common observation.

mouldings with the characteristic *fillet* on the more prominent members—a particular of detail deserving of remark, as it constitutes a distinguishing feature in the style of architecture now under consideration, and is seen in great variety of position, and to the utmost advantage throughout the design of the Wakefield Chantry.

The roof reposed its weight upon the walls without the assistance either of side brackets in the piers of the windows or tie-beams.

The latter would have interfered with the arch of the Altar window, though raised upon the summit of the projecting stone cornice by which the walls on the inside are terminated.

The beams and rafters in the course of time, and in consequence of neglect, were destroyed, and replaced by others to which strength alone was given.

The present roof is certainly of considerable age; it is of English oak, massy and plain, with a tie-beam, king-post, and struts, the archetype of the truss now in common use; it is covered with stone slabs, and has, partly by these means, become too heavy for the side walls, which from several concomitant causes· incline outwards—a result in no way surprising when the slenderness of their substance, sixteen inches, is considered.

But even the west wall, the most substantial of the four, has yielded to successive injuries; the bond in the masonry has been intersected, a mischief which, in addition to the fractures occasioned by a settlement, and extending longitudinally through the centre of its bulk, has seriously crippled this important part of the edifice.

The construction is peculiar in many points, owing no doubt to the limited dimensions of the building, and the unusual form of its basement.

The bond in a thin wall can neither be so regular nor so secure as in one more solid; but still the original strength was sufficient: and it may safely be declared, that if the Chapel had been protected from extreme violence, its strength and beauty would have remained, in all essential respects, unimpaired.

The care manifested in loading the walls so that only a due weight should press on the basement, is a merit in the design and construction of this building to which too much praise cannot be given.

The consequence of reducing the side walls to comparative lightness is apparent in the jambs of the windows, which have sufficient breadth of moulding, but very little recess or depth on either side.

Substance of wall is required more for the purpose of carrying into execution the *retreating character*, or graduated arrangement of several planes one beyond another in the formation of all openings, than for strength; and this is observable in all the architecture of England before the commencement of the thirteenth century, after which period it was abandoned, and the members were blended together, still however retaining the aggregate depth in an elaborate series of mouldings.

The narrow space in the instance before us prevented their expansion; but in others, where no slender limit was assigned to the thickness of the walls and arches, and full freedom was used in spreading the mouldings through a great portion of their substance, the system was worked out with admirable skill.

The southern angle of the west front leans considerably towards the west, and its recovery to an erect position will require the utmost care, and the temporary removal of at least the shaft which crowns the summit.

The oblique direction of this elegant feature most probably occasioned the fall of its lofty pinnacle.

The accident at this angle of the building is not of modern date, and no perceptible increase of it has taken place within the last forty years.

The north-west angle was in a far worse condition before the last general repairs were made to prevent this part of the building from falling.

The defects on the outside are tolerably well concealed, but strong evidences remain on the inside, of the severity of the fractures.

The remains of the turret prove that it once rose from the parapet in the same figure and proportions as the corresponding one at the south-west angle, and that, like it, the four sides were recessed, the pedestals of the niches being incorporated with the canopies of other niches terminating the angle buttresses.

The pinnacles are the crowning members of the clustered canopies.

Their original height is determined by the breadth and slope of the base which forms the solid of the canopies, around which are thickly gathered the exquisite ornaments which once protected the statues.

A peculiarity in the position of the crockets on the lower pinnacles of the angle buttresses, claims particular notice.

These ornaments generally spring from the edges, but in the instances before us, are attached to the alternate *faces* of the octagons.

The effect is scarcely less ornamental or less pleasing than the design is novel.

The tie between the north and west walls is completely severed, the gap being several inches wide.

These facts account for the dilapidated state of the parapet, as seen in the prints before referred to, and for its restoration as it now appears, after the substructure had been strengthened to support the weight.

The view in the "Vale of Bolton" must again be referred to. It distinctly represents the projection of the two extreme buttresses of the west front as considerably bolder than the rest; and the accuracy of the drawing is placed beyond question by the appearance of the mutilated buttress near the southern angle of the beautiful original : if the south face of this buttress be examined just above the modern stonework, it will be seen that *one half* of a panel, with its elegantly disposed tracery, and a finial on the angle of the upper or retreating member of the same buttress, are still remaining.

This panel completed, gives the buttress its due and proper prominency.

Upon Cawthorn's authority, supported by that of Mr. Lumb, attention may be directed to the lower portions of the larger buttresses which flank the elevation, and are *panelled*.

These in the building are now made quite plain, and reduced in bulk for the same reason that may be assigned for the utter defacement of the lower part of the entire facade, namely, the want of space on the bridge.

The four smaller buttresses in the front, terminating in crocketed pediments above the battlements, are no longer remaining; nor is the finial which, thirty years ago, surmounted the ogee canopy within the pediment over the centre doorway.

The exquisite design and proportion of the east elevation are still conspicuous, unsparingly as ruin has lighted upon its fair turrets, magnificent window, and graceful parapet.

The latter was elevated in the form of a gable (indicated by Cawthorn and others), the inclination of which corresponded with the stone cornice on the inside.

The form of the head of the east window, a portion of which still remains, is determined by the cornice: the side labels descending from its mouldings, are still discernible on the inside.

Notwithstanding the barbarous injuries which have been inflicted on the interior wall of the elegant staircase-turret, and the removal of several of the stone steps, with the newel, this appendage, as well as the whole of the east front of the Chapel with which it is connected, remains as erect as it was left by the original builders, and needs only the restitution of those members of which it has been deprived, to perfect its solidity and good appearance.

The east window consisted of five compartments. Cawthorn's print alone supplies a hint for any part of the design; slender as it is it becomes useful, and agrees with the character exemplified by the lateral windows, in the main divisions of the space into side arches deriving their mouldings from those of the jambs and mullions, and leaving a broad centre for a superior or more varied pattern of tracery.

The six smaller windows on the sides were uniform, very handsome, and of three compartments.

The highest testimony of their splendour is preserved by Mr. Lumb in a drawing of the Chapel, made by himself about forty years since, borne out by Fleming's venerable engraving.

The beautiful design of the windows, as represented in the annexed woodcut, and their highly-wrought mouldings, are still vividly remembered by Mr. Lumb, whose memoranda in reference to these features are most valuable.

The present windows, with their wretched substitutes for mullions and tracery, are named merely because they retain the form and position of the pointed arch in the original design; but the peculiar partition of this arch, by which the pattern of the tracery becomes disconnected, is alone to be found in the drawing above referred to.

It may be well to observe, that the subdivision of the arch in this manner is not singular in the design of the Chantry: the same kind of tracery is presented by the arches between the doors, and in the fronts of the two extreme buttresses at the west end.

The square form of these windows, and the pedimental shape of the east window, rarely appear in the style of this period.

But even in still earlier architecture the same shapes sometimes occur, as instanced in the Chancel of Skipwith Church, Yorkshire; and perhaps for the same reason as may be assigned for their introduction in this Chapel—the want of space for arches of sufficient magnitude; for had the arches been detached from their frames, the appearance of their having been forced into a space not lofty enough to receive them, could not have been avoided; but by reducing the arch to a secondary feature, so as to combine with the tracery, the enclosing frame may fairly be carried up, as in this instance, to the cornice, with which it ranges in parallel lines, and make the increased extent of enrichment, thus pro-

vided in the windows, appear in just proportion
to that of the rest of the design.

The exact section of the mouldings of the
interior labels of the windows may be ascertained from fragments, which, having been
wrought on the same blocks of stone as those
forming the cornice, could not, without more
trouble than was deemed necessary, be wholly
obliterated by the destroyers.

This character of suspending the labels from
the cornice is maintained in every instance,
inside and out.

Their length is half the height of the windows, including the corbels, of which no in-
telligible trace remains on the inside.

The authors have observed the careless remark in the " Beauties of England and Wales,"
that the "*parapets are perforated;*" but as there
is no record in writing of earlier date than the
indisputably authentic drawing already so often
quoted, and as this valuable document, by shew-
ing a fragment attached to the octagonal turret,
advances a firm step towards proof that the
parapets were panelled with a succession of solid
compartments, they base their ideas upon the
highest authority within their reach.

The parapet, as expressed by Mr. Lumb, is
certainly incomplete, and was most probably
originally surmounted by battlements, in accord-

ance with those on the west front; and it seems most likely that the equivocal term used in the above work was intended to describe the embrasures between them.

The present termination has always been regarded as a coarse and unskilful imitation of the ancient, in the execution of which no attempt was made to restore the original model, the object alone being to furnish the building with the best appearance, at the least possible cost.

Its height is three feet ten inches and a half, but a considerably greater addition would have been required for a pierced summit.

Had any trace of a finishing ornament of the kind remained, it would surely have been remarked by Mr. Lumb, who knew the Chapel well, many years before the hasty description penned for the " Beauties" was committed to the press. But the whole description of the design of the Chapel is not merely worthless, it is mischievous, inasmuch as it leads those who, having neither eyes nor understanding of their own, repeat errors which the most ordinary observation would detect and set aside.

" Gothic, or Saracenic Architecture"—" East window overhanging the river," and " perforated parapets," are statements not warranted

by facts, and must be despised by all who are
unwilling to be misguided.

And yet these glaring inaccuracies have been
reprinted in modern publications of value and
importance.

———

The sculpture in the marvellous design of
the west front is of the most interesting description.

The five divisions in the parapet were filled
with subjects derived from the inspired narra-
tives of the sacred life of our Saviour, flanked
at each extremity by six whole-length statues
in niches in two tiers, forming with their lofty
canopies the summits of the buttresses.

The statues have been demolished, but the
sculptures wrought in the solid blocks forming
the parapet have escaped, except with the loss
of limbs and features, of which latter time
chiefly has deprived them.

These sculptures were wholly worked after
the parapet was built, and, as was not unfrequently the case, left incomplete.

The first in order, but the one reserved to
the last for the sculptor's art, was designed
for the reception of a representation of the
Annunciation.

The block is slightly roughed out for the figures of St. Gabriel and the Blessed Virgin.

This was a favourite subject formerly, and its frequent introduction shews the fervour of the pious adoration with which our forefathers viewed the divine condescension and mercy manifested in the Holy Incarnation.

It may be seen twice repeated on the porch of the gateway of Radford Abbey, Nottinghamshire; on the front of the tower of Banwell Church, Somersetshire; and among the ruins of Rievaulx Abbey.

The Annunciation is also represented on the tower gateway of St. Mary's or New College, Oxford, as well as within the quadrangles; and was the first of a series of highly-relieved figures in the choir, over the Altar, illustrative of the same five prominent mysteries as those selected for the edification of the devout at Wakefield.

The ancient statuary referred to at Oxford, together with the richly-carved and painted screens, and the oaken stall-work—the spoils of the Chapel, were huddled together in the tower, where they remained until thirty years since, when they were rescued for a time from further indignity, by the good taste of the Reverend Dr. Penrose, but the ledge which he caused to be fixed for their reception against one of the walls of the cloisters, has lately been removed, and the sculptures, together with the tablet commemorative of their sacrilegious treatment, are now deposited near the floor, preparatory to their extermination, which seems likely soon to follow the mutilations already recommenced and invited by their present exposure.

FRAGMENTA · HÆC
ALTARIS · IN · MVRO · CAPELLÆ · TRANSVERSALI
A · FVNDATORE · EXTRVCTI
IVSSV · ROB · HORNE · EPISC · WINT · SÆCVLO · XVI
DEMOLITI.

———

CVSTOS · ET · SCHOLARES · HVIVS · COLLEGII
HIC · TANDEM · COLLOCANDA
CVRAVERVNT.
ANNO · CIↃ IↃ CCC XIV

As a comparative description of the New College Sculptures with those in front of the Chapel at Wakefield may prove interesting, the authors subjoin the following remarks upon their respective distinctions.

I. The Annunciation.

NEW COLLEGE.

St. Mary stands in a dignified posture, yet full of humility and grace, holding an open book in her left hand, being visited in that private preparation of heart by which she became fitted for the fulfilment of the Divine promise.

The flourishing emblem of purity occupies the middle of the panel, and the messenger of the joyful tidings concerning the Incarnation of God the Son, approaches in an attitude of obeisance indicative of his profound reverence and admiration in the presence of the Blessed Virgin, whom he greets with the angelical salutation.

WAKEFIELD BRIDGE-CHAPEL.

The stone beneath the triple canopy was merely prepared to receive the sculpture.

II. The Holy Nativity.

The infant Saviour rests on the right arm of his highly favoured mother, who is ex-

Our Saviour is supported on the right arm of St. Mary, who reclines on a kind of

SCULPTURE IN THE CENTRAL COMPARTMENT OF THE WEST FRONT.

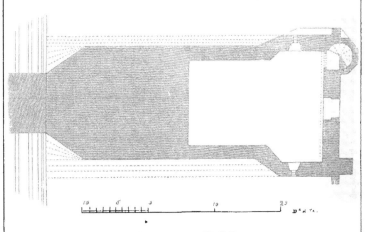

PLAN OF THE BASEMENT

ten ... ... in front ro... ...
... and across ...
... to the ancle... ... pa...
... are lying ... ...
... enclosure.

Towards the feet... ... ...
... chair, sits tw... ...
... of the Blessed Virg...

II. The Christ's ...

The Redeemer is rising ... ... Ang...
of the tomb, and in fro... ... ...
two completely armed soldiers ... ...
... starting up in confu... ... ...
... zement.

... ...
... ...
... ...
... ...
... ...

IV. The Ascension ...

The figure of our Saviour ...
emerges from the clo... ... ...
received him out of human ...
sight.

In ... are two kneeling ...
figures with minds, and their ...
hands raised, as if to hide ...
their faces from the brightness of his glory; and on
either side the beholders, all
having minds, with uplifted
hands.

The contour of the figures,

E ..

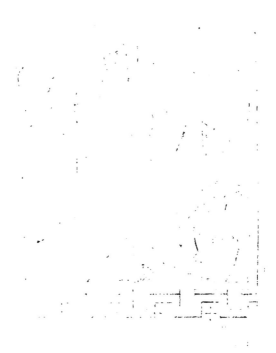

NEW COLLEGE.

tended on a couch, in front of which an ox and an ass, according to the ancient tradition, are lying within a hurdled enclosure.

Towards the feet, and in a wattled chair, sits the chaste spouse of the Blessed Virgin.

WAKEFIELD BRIDGE CHAPEL.

rustic couch, with her head resting on a tasselled cushion.

St. Joseph is seen at her feet, and in the background the two animals in front of the rack; whilst the announcing Angel appears overhead.

III. The Glorious Resurrection of our Lord.

The Redeemer is rising out of the tomb, and in front, two completely armed soldiers are starting up in confused amazement.

A kneeling Angel is represented on each side of the rising figure; and beneath, three guards, set to keep watch over the monument, clad as knights, and holding heater-shaped shields, terrified by the vision and earthquake.

IV. The Ascension of our Blessed Lord.

The figure of our Saviour emerges from the cloud which received Him out of human sight.

In front are two kneeling figures with nimbs, and their hands raised, as if to hide their faces from the brightness of His glory; and on either side the beholders, all having nimbs, with uplifted hands.

The contour of these figures,

The lower part of the figure of our Saviour fills the centre canopy; beneath, His holy Apostles, six seated in front, and five behind, are gazing upward in attitudes of astonishment.

tion of
as illus
of her h

ped, as
the les, and
a back; t
ged is ved, leaving
the tly open
at ated with
d he quatref as
spe new solv
n as
are represented
the figures sit
t the tomb,
St. distinguished
by a

SCULPTURE IN THE FIFTH COMPARTMENT OF THE WEST FRONT

It is unknown to whom the full length statues which occupied the twelve elevated niches in the front of the Chapel at Wakefield, referred.

Two of them were pre-eminently distinguished by their size and situation, and are likely to have represented St. Anne and St. Joachim.

The pedestals upon which they stood, remain in every instance, variously formed and ornamented, and several upheld by Angels with expanded wings.

The subjects just described cannot but be regarded as masterly specimens of sculptural design, and were not the only portions reserved for the finer finish of detail till after the erection of the structure.

Probably the whole of the ornamental carving, the greater part of which is of the most delicate description, was produced upon a roughened surface; for unless this had been the case the accuracy of the jointings could not have been preserved; and the process would at once account for a small space left incomplete in the *diaper* over the middle doorway[g].

[g] The term diaper seems clearly applicable to the peculiar kind of decoration referred to.

It is in fact, a *surface ornament*, employed to obliterate blank spaces of stone-work in Churches, screens, or monuments designed to exhibit more than usual care in the enrichment; and is variously applied on the outside and inside of the buildings of all periods.

The practice mentioned was more common anciently than it is now, but whatever the system by which so much exquisite enrichment was incorporated with the design, the wonder is that the stone ·on which it was thus elaborately executed, should so long have resisted the attacks of time.

The writers dwell not with admiration upon the *quantity* of ornament in the design, but rather upon the pure and refined taste exercised in its selection and execution.

Nothing grotesque in conception nor coarse in workmanship is observable. All the forms are genuine, and such as pertain to the best specimens of the architecture of the period.

Foliage has supplied a rich variety of patterns, to the exclusion of other models so often and so elegantly appropriated to ecclesiastical architecture.

Heraldry could not find room for so much as

The doors at Much Wymondley in Hertfordshire, and Chipping Ongar in Essex; the nave of Rochester Cathedral, the approach to the undercroft at Canterbury, and the tower of St. Ethelbert belonging to the Monastery of St. Augustine, present good specimens in the Norman style.

Among later, the interior of Westminster Abbey, the choir and Chapter House of Canterbury Cathedral, Waltham Cross, the high altar screen in Selby Abbey, the rood screen in Lincoln Cathedral, the monument of Gervase Alard, in Winchelsea Church, Sussex, and that of Bishop Hatfield at Durham, may be named on account of the beauty of their diaper-work.

a single device in any part of the building,
unless indeed we may suppose it to have been
employed for the enrichment of the stone corbels, or the carved wood-work in the interior,
and to have disappeared with the features to
which it was attached.

The architecture of the fourteenth century
was in general rich in ornament of the kind;
Abbey Churches as well as Cathedrals frequently present a vast variety of armorial em-
blems ; but it may be that the founder of this
Chapel purposely excluded a kind of memorial which, in many cases, has remained to
identify benefactors with the monuments of
their piety after other tradition or record had
perished.

Modern architects are taught a valuable lesson
by this beautiful structure.

They will observe that the ornaments throughout its design are subservient to the main constituent features.

Its author was obedient, comparatively di-
minutive as was the scale upon which he was
employed, to this established principle, which
was scrupulously observed until invaded and
almost subverted by the preponderating in-
fluence of ornament towards the latter end of
the fifteenth century.

In the present example, which so finely illustrates the system just referred to, the buttresses, pediments, arches, in short the *outline* of the design, viewed in connexion with the highly ornamented surface of the wall, is exhibited in strong relief.

A blank superficies is not to be seen in the west front, and yet there is no want of solidity in its appearance, so admirably have the ornaments been made to assist as well as enrich the effect of the general design.

The comparatively modern restoration of some of the ornamental work before alluded to, remains to be further noticed.

Several of the canopies in the parapet, and of the battlements which surmount it, may be ascribed to the first general repairs of the Chapel made sometime in the seventeenth century.

There is some merit in these imitations, but their juxtaposition with genuine specimens forces an unfavourable comparison.

The coarse stone in which they are executed has however been well attached to the ancient work, and thus far we view it as a successful example of the process of repair.

Before closing the remarks upon this most interesting part of the building, it is to be observed that the straight line of battlement which terminates the front, is strictly in keep-

ing, true as it is that in the thirteenth and
fourteenth centuries, steep gables were usually
characteristic of the edifices of the age.

The omission of this feature in the present
instance, and the repetition of the horizontal
line throughout the elevation, relieved only by
prominent buttresses, and aspiring pinnacles,
was doubtless maintained to preserve such a
harmony in the design as certainly no other
form could have rendered more completely
elegant.

The furniture, by having been swept from
the Chantry upon its suppression, leaves to con-
jecture the probable partition of the interior,
and the order of the seats on the sides.

These, separated by an avenue in the
centre, were ranged between the screen at
the lower end, and the Sanctuary or Altarpace, which was raised above the floor by a
single step.

In the choirs of cathedral, monastic, colle-
giate, and parish Churches, as in college
Chapels, the stalls for the clergy were invariably arranged in lines parallel with the side
walls, while the seats for the laity in the nave,
were placed in the opposite direction, or facing
the east.

The oaken stall-work in the Chapel of St.
John's Hospital, now used as the Grammar

School, in Coventry, may be named as one of the most entire specimens now remaining.

These magnificent stalls were removed from the Church of the Grey Friars, and must have completely furnished a choir of vast extent. They are as old as the commencement of the fourteenth century, and seem to have escaped injury until their exposure to mischief in their present situation.

The screen, extending across the width of the Chapel, and parting off ten or twelve feet in length from the west end, determined the ante-chapel or vestibule—a free and very useful space in this kind of building, and one without which due order could not at all times have been preserved, as the doors were seldom closed, nor the place unoccupied, though there were intervals in the regular services.

The Janitor was present to bestow the accustomed alms, and issue written orders to certify at the gate of the Monastery in view, or the Hospital on the way, the arrival of worthy travellers from the Wayside Chapel.

The stone seat he occupied is formed in the west wall, between two of the doors: it is a handsome feature of the original design, having had side buttresses, and a crocketed canopy nearly resembling those of the niches in the buttresses of the west front.

The Altar formerly attached to the east wall
has been destroyed[h].

A small but very beautiful panel, hemmed in
with modern masonry, is the only ornamental
fragment of the piscina, now remaining. It
occupies its original position beneath the recess,
at the back of which was a little window of two
compartments, whose former existence is only
known by an original drawing in the Bodleian
Library.

No traces are observable either of a sedilis
on the south side of the Sanctuary or of a stoup
at the west end : these were not unfrequently
moveable articles of furniture ; the one a seat
of wood for the officiating priest, the other a
small vessel of metal for the water of puri-
fication to be used on entering the chapel.

The beautiful character of the niche at the
east end, and on the south side of the Altar, is
indicated by the state of the wall from which
the lofty pinnacles, the tall and tapering canopy,

[h] As the remains of Norman altars are very rare, it may be well
to observe that a curious relic of this kind and age is preserved in
the garden of the rectory-house at Dunham Magna, in Norfolk.

It consists of a large portion of the top stone, five inches in thickness, finished with mouldings, and enriched with the indented star-
ornament.

When perfect it measured about five feet nine inches in length,
and three feet one inch in width, and was impressed with the five
small crosses.

and the elevated pedestal, have been sacrilegiously chipped away.

The overhanging form of the canopy is shewn by the upper part of the recess, which was ribbed in an elaborate pattern over the head of the statue of St. Mary.

The recess in the north wall, over the Altarpace, may at first sight be conjectured to have been designed for an ambry, but its antiquity, as well as its purpose, must be acknowledged equally uncertain : the masonry is quite rough, and the depth very irregular.

If it were ever graced with enrichments worthy its position, these, with the label and all the accompanying mouldings, have been removed, and the opening filled to the surface.

The absence of capitals as crowning members of the jambs and mullions, may be remarked as uncommon ; nothing of the kind occurs in any part of the Chapel.

Economy in space obliged the uprights of the doors to be singularly narrow, but they are deeply recessed, and formed of numerous mouldings, which are continued on the arches without interruption at the springer.

As there are no capitals, no members in the design are to be distinguished as columns or pillars, names usually assigned to a torus, however slender, wherever it is distinguished with capital and base.

Traces of painting are still discernible upon the walls in the interior.

The enrichments of the architecture left but few blank spaces for decorations of this kind, but these, whatever their extent, and probably also the whole interior surface,—mouldings, sculptures, and windows, were formerly covered with fresco, which was in high perfection in England during the fourteenth century.

Gilding was added to enrich its effect, and harmonize in splendour with the painted glass.

It seems surprising that hands were found mischievous enough to commence and carry on the work of spoliation in a little Wayside Asylum like this, so exquisitely beautiful in all its finishings, and which had been so long devoted to sacred purposes; but its costlier appurtenances, the gold and silver with which the Altar was doubtless graced, were irresistible; these brought down desecration and destruction upon the building; and what the rapacity of former times spared, has been ignorantly reduced in later, and a crippled shell remains to prove the taste and liberality of the present age in the work of restoration.

The consolation which has carried the writers somewhat patiently through an examination

Lightning Source UK Ltd.
Milton Keynes UK
UKOW06n2111050816

280071UK00001B/17/P